I WANT TO BE READY

I WANT TO BE READY

Sheron C. Patterson

Abingdon Press
Nashville

I WANT TO BE READY

Copyright © 1994 by Abingdon Press

This book is printed on acid-free, recycled paper.

Library of Congress Cataloging-in-Publication Data

Patterson, Sheron C., 1962-
  I want to be ready / Sheron C. Patterson.
    p.   cm.
  ISBN 0-687-24133-2
  1. Afro-Americans—Quotations. 2. Meditations. I. Title.
PN 6081.3.P38   1994
818'.02—dc20
                                                              94-898
                                                              CIP

Scripture quotations are from the New Revised Standard Version Bible, copyright © 1989, by the Division of Christian Education of the National Council of the Churches of Christ in the United States of America.

The lines on page 36 are from "Lift Every Voice and Sing" by James Weldon Johnson and J. Rosamond Johnson. Copyright 1927 Edward B. Marks Music Corporation. Used by permission of Edward B. Marks Music Company.

The lines on page 48 are from *And Still I Rise* by Maya Angelou. Copyright © 1978 by Maya Angelou. Reprinted by permission of Random House, Inc.

96 97 98 99 00 01 02 03 — 10 9 8 7 6 5 4

MANUFACTURED IN THE UNITED STATES OF AMERICA

This book is dedicated to my sons,
Robert, Jr. and Christian

Introduction

We are a people of the Word. God's word has been a "lamp to [our] feet and a light to [our] path," ever since our beginnings in this country. Also the words spoken by influential members of our community have shaped our actions for centuries. This book combines both of these precious elements with the purpose of providing a spiritual and cultural environment for meditation.

Each of these fifty meditations is designed to help Christians live an abundant life in our contemporary society. The topics include racial pride, the role of faith, and concerns for our young people.

Allow these meditations to usher you into a greater spiritual and cultural enrichment.

There is a use for almost everything.

—George Washington Carver

Describing our ancestors as resourceful is like calling fire hot. They seemed effortlessly to take a little bit of nothing and make a whole lot of something.

Carver was one of those resourceful people. He looked around his world and saw a meaningful use for many things. He possessed a spirit of creativity that had no boundaries.

So it is with God. A long time ago our Lord took a large mass of nothing and created our world. God's spirit of creativity is still alive now. Daily, God looks around this world, and sees value in everybody and everything. God specializes in using cast-off, thrown-away people. Even though the world can routinely devalue us, God is constantly there to declare us invaluable and use us for heaven's sake.

Can you value all those who are around you?

Dear God, I have a purpose in this world. Use me to your glory. Amen.

For further meditation read Genesis 1:1-31.

No race can prosper till it learns that there is as much dignity in tilling a field as in writing a poem.

—Booker T. Washington

Status-hungry and materialistic. Those words all too often describe our world. Superficial issues such as the type of car a person drives, or the amount of money in his or her bank account, supersedes the desire to know who the person is inside.

A long time ago, Washington realized that everyone can make a contribution to the world, regardless of one's outer trappings and possessions. Washington realized that even though we are all different, we can be united in our differences. If we didn't, the race would stumble.

In the same way, Christians are called to work together within the body of Christ. If we don't work together, the church fails. We all have a responsibility to do the best we can at whatever we can. The eyes must see. The feet must walk. The various parts don't have time for jealousy or snobbery. They must work together.

Can you focus on the success of the whole, rather than on the status of the parts?

Dear God, free me from excessive worry about what someone else has. Place my mind on unity and community. Amen.

For further meditation read 1 Corinthians 12:12-26.

I would crawl on my hands and knees, through mud and mire, to the feet of a learned man, where I would sit and humbly supplicate him to instill into me that which neither devils nor tyrants could remove, only with my life—for colored people to acquire learning in this country makes tyrants quake and tremble on their sandy foundation.

—David Walker

When education was forbidden we longed for it. Our ancestors craved knowledge as parched souls in a desert thirst after water. The risks of education were fierce. Lashes or even lynchings were in store for those caught in the act of learning. Yet they risked and took chances because they believed that knowledge would transform them into better people.

Like them, we also should yearn for the knowledge of God. We need to learn about God in order to live lives of power and might. As the scripture says, we should hunger not just for bread, but for "every word that comes from the mouth of the LORD."

Dear God, I come before you like an empty pitcher before a full fountain. Fill me. Amen.

For further meditation read Deuteronomy 8:3.

It is time for everyone of us to roll up our sleeves and put ourselves at the top of our commitment list.

—Marion Wright Edelman

If I don't watch out, I'll find myself dishing up hugs, kisses, and warm fuzzies for a cast of thousands. There seems to be enough affection to satisfy church members, family, friends, and even an enemy or two. But sometimes love for myself is the last thing on my mind.

Wright Edelman has a point in urging us to roll up our sleeves in order to begin to love ourselves. Sometimes it is hard work to stop and concentrate on the self. Try it. Pat yourself on the back. Hug yourself. Blow yourself a kiss in the mirror.

One of the best reasons to love ourselves is that we are temples of the Lord. The Holy Spirit dwells in us. This makes us very special in the sight of God. According to the scriptures, you are holy.

Can you do something loving for yourself today?

Dear God, keep me mindful of my life as a temple of your Holy Spirit. Help me remember continually to love myself. Amen.

For further meditation read 1 Corinthians 3:16-17.

I'd tell the white powers that I ain't trying to take nothing from them. I'm trying to make Mississippi a better place for all of us. And I'd say, "What you don't understand is that as long as you stand with your feet on my neck, you got to stand in a ditch too. But if you move, I'm coming out. I want to get us both out of the ditch."

—Fannie Lou Hamer

Coming up out of ditches is not a solo act. Both the oppressor and the oppressed should come up and out together. Simultaneously, feet should lift off of necks and knees should spring up out of the dirt.

We won't come up out of the ditches together until we realize that we are together in the ditches. Whether we like it or not, we are connected to one another. Even though we may live on opposing sides, we are our brothers' and sisters' keeper. Our lives are intertwined.

Can you see brotherhood and sisterhood in the ditches of your life and climb out with the one you oppressed or who oppressed you?

Dear God, strengthen the ties that bind me to others in the ditches of my life. Bring us up and out together. Amen.

For further meditation read Genesis 4:9.

The real problem is not the bad guys, it is the good guys have gone to sleep.

—Maynard Jackson

Jesus awakened the slumbering disciples with the riveting question, "Are you still sleeping?" Fatigue had gripped their eyelids and rendered them incapable of watching and praying through the night. Their answer had to have been an embarrassed *yes*.

Instead of sleeping, they could have been vigilant on behalf of Jesus. So it is with us. We spiritually sleep when Jesus needs us wide awake. We catnap when we could be called into active duty. We doze when we should be disciples.

There is much for us to do in our communities, churches, and homes. The Lord may be calling you right now to the task of mentoring or volunteering, or tutoring and leading. To hear the call, we must be alert, committed, and disciplined.

Are you ready to serve the Lord?

Dear God, wake me up and show me what you would have me do in your world. Amen.

For further meditation read Matthew 26:44-46.

The major threat to blacks in America has not been oppression, but rather the loss of hope and absence of meaning.

—Cornel West

Something mighty powerful kept a smile on my dad's face every day when I was a small girl. I did not know it back then, but he was enduring racial harassment on his job. As one of the first African American police officers in our city, he daily ran a gauntlet of cruel and unceasing verbal and physical hate.

I never knew he was in pain. All I saw was a man with a demeanor of hope and a purpose in life. As I matured I learned that his encounters were not unique. They were just a part of the African American experience in this country.

However, I am thankful for the other part of our experience—a God who continuously fills us with hope. Without hope, oppression is lethal. Hope keeps us moving forward when we'd just as soon give up. Hope makes us smile at tomorrow, even though today is a bitter pill.

Hope is an "anchor of the soul." A hopeless soul is a major threat to the body.

Is your hope anchored in the Lord?

Dear God, give me hope when I face oppression. Amen.

For further meditation read Hebrews 6:19.

You cannot fight by being on the outside complaining and whining. You have to get on the inside to be able to assess their strengths and weaknesses and then move in.

—Shirley Chisholm

Jesus was never one to sit back and complain or whine. He came into this world, examined the situation, and worked for positive changes. His method was successful. If we follow his lead we can be too, but it takes guts.

A move from the outside to the inside of the problems that confront us requires bravery. It is easier to talk than it is to act. Shirley Chisholm surveyed her world and decided to move in and make a change.

We've been given a gift of bravery. Jesus has promised us even more power than he possessed if we can believe in him.

Can you move toward your problems, rather than away from them?

Dear God, strengthen me to tackle my problems, rather than just talk about them. Amen.

For further meditation read John 14:12.

If you're going to play the game properly, you'd better know every rule.

—Barbara Jordan

Search all you want to, but there are no shortcuts, quick fixes, or magic potions that lead to heaven. Jesus Christ is the only way in. He is the truth, the light, and the pathway to God.

One day a rich young ruler approached Jesus and inquired of the guidelines. Jesus concisely stated, "Sell your possessions, and give the money to the poor, and you will have treasure in heaven; then come, follow me." The young man realized that he could not be a part of what Jesus offered because he could not follow the rules.

Life is surely not a game, but there are guidelines that help us live advantageously. Knowledge of these guidelines is precious and challenging. They lead to a blessed existence.

Can you follow Jesus' rules?

Dear God, teach me your rules and help me live by them every day. Amen.

For further meditation read Matthew 19:16-23.

If folk can learn to be racist, then they can learn to be antiracist. If being a sexist ain't genetic, then dad gum, people can learn about gender equality.

—Johnetta B. Cole

What a shock it must have been for the disciples to stumble upon Jesus conversing with a Samaritan woman. Perhaps their eyes bugged and their mouths gaped open at the sight. From their perspective their Savior had gone too far. He was talking to a woman in public!

Jesus knew that all humans have an intrinsic worth and value. He knew that men are not superior to women. Sure, his actions rocked the boat. He was not afraid to demonstrate his beliefs before all. In fact, he acted out his beliefs before the world in order to change the world.

Our challenge is to be more like him. If you are like Jesus, you'll look at a person and see neither gender nor race nor class. If you're like Jesus, folk may talk about you because of your righteous living. If you're like Jesus, it won't matter—you've got more important things to do than hate.

Do you want to be like Jesus?

Dear God, free me from racial, gender, and economic prejudice. Those are burdens that weigh me down. Amen.

For further meditation read John 4:7-29.

If you don't know where you came from, it's difficult to assess where you are. It's even more difficult to plan where you are going.

—Joseph Lowery

The African man traveling down the Gaza road was in turmoil. He wanted to be a Christian, but he didn't know much about the religion. Even though he possessed a Bible, it was of little use to him. Without a knowledge of the word of God, he had no place for his faith to take root.

He was lost until he encountered Philip, who preached Jesus to him. From that point the African gained direction and purpose. The word of God was like a compass in his life. It was an indicator of where he should start, where he should be, and where he needed to go.

We also need God's direction in our lives. God is willing to be our beginning, present, and ending as well, if we allow the holy words to touch our hearts.

Will you follow God's lead?

Dear God, place within me your divine compass, so that as long as you are in me I know where I am and where I am going. Amen.

For further meditation read Acts 8:4-40.

Thoughts have power. Thoughts are energy. And you can make your world or break your world by your thinking.

—Susan L. Taylor

The unnamed sick woman with the hemorrhage must have been thinking some powerfully positive thoughts the day she encountered Jesus. It would have been so easy for her to give up. She'd been sick for twelve years. But despite the pain, the woman appeared to have kept her mind on the uplifting ideas.

Only positive thoughts could have motivated her to get out of the house and find Jesus. Depression would have kept her tucked under the covers, moaning and pathetic. Her thoughts lifted her beyond her current limitations and led her to the Lord.

Positive thoughts can make a difference in our lives as well. Despair and depression shut us down, whereas positive thoughts keep hope in action.

Can you allow positive thoughts to lift you?

Dear God, fill my mind with positive thoughts so I can handle whatever life throws my way. Amen.

For further meditation read Luke 8:43-48.

In life, if you have a purpose in which you can believe, there's no end to the amount of things you can accomplish.

—Marian Anderson

Imagine what life must have been like for the biblical character who built his house on sand, rather than on solid rock. He was living on shaky ground. Doubt and confusion probably colored his existence.

However, the other man who built his house on solid rock had a sure foundation. He'd built on the permanent. His future undoubtedly felt more secure. A permanent foundation for a home functions much as God does for the soul. If you plant your hopes there, all things are possible.

We've come a long way as a people due to lives built on the solid rock. We all should embrace this blessed legacy. All other ground is sinking sand.

Is your life built on a foundation you can depend on?

Dear God, help me stand on you and not myself or the things of this world. Amen.

For further meditation read Matthew 7:24-27.

Nothing the future brings can defeat a people who have come through three hundred years of slavery and humiliation and privation with heads high and eyes clear and straight.

—Paul Robeson

Man-made trouble means nothing to our God. Those who believe this, act like it. They are confident, calm, and secure in the face of danger. They know, sooner or later, that the Lord will make a way.

Our history exemplifies this. Despite centuries of slavery, we can hold our heads high because we serve a God of victory.

The Psalmist seems to possess this calmness too. He predicts that troubles will come, but they will pass, and in the end God will allow his head to be lifted up above his enemies.

Can the past victories of your people strengthen you to handle today's problems?

Dear God, free me from the painful shackles that seek to shame me. Allow historical victories to be sources of strength. Amen.

For further meditation read Psalm 27:1-3.

Given the odds, we weren't supposed to stop being slaves. Given the opposition, we weren't supposed to have an education. Given the history, we weren't supposed to have families. Given the blues, we weren't supposed to have spirit. Given the power of the enemy, we weren't supposed to fight back. Not only have we achieved victories, we have—despite the powers against us—become our own victories.

—Camille Cosby

We serve an "anyway" God. Impediments, hurdles and obstacles are our inheritance, yet we excelled anyway. Kidnapped from Africa, enslaved and shackled, stripped of our culture, robbed of our native language, torn from our family units, today we thrive anyway.

Surely the Lord was in the midst of our past, at work to usher us into a better day. The evidence that the Lord kept us, in the face of horrific conditions, is simply too great to deny.

Even today, life for us is no cakewalk, but the fact that we walk at all is due to God, who conquers anyhow.

Can you recognize and celebrate the presence of God in your good and bad times?

Dear God, no matter how high the odds are stacked against me, I can overcome with you. Amen.

For further meditation read 2 Corinthians 6:4-10.

Lifting as they climb, onward and upward they go, struggling and striving and hoping that the buds and blossoms of their desires may burst into glorious fruition ere long.

—Mary Church Terrell

The largest crowd is always at the bottom of the ladder, not the top. Our challenge is to reach back and to help others up. Long denied access to the ladder, a sense of community must urge us to seize the rungs together. Each one must reach one.

Terrell realized that just being able to climb the ladder was a mighty blessing. And our blessings should never exist in isolation. They deserve communal exposure.

When was the last time you lifted someone on your way up?

Dear God, keep me mindful of those who follow behind me. Remind me to reach back and lift them as I press on. Amen.

For further meditation read Philippians 3:14.

It is impossible to love ourselves without having an affection for Africa.

—Randall Robinson

God does not make mistakes, humans do. We are not of African descent by accident. God planned it that way. Our African roots are a gift from God.

A portion of our American history includes the denial of our African heritage, and the attempt to forget our origins.

If we as a people are ever authentically to love ourselves, we must love our whole selves. This includes a love for our ebony-hued skin, tight curly hair, wide noses, and thick lips. Dark and lovely we are; African-born and blessed of God we are.

Can you feel love for your gift of African heritage?

Dear God, I praise you for who I am on the inside and on the outside. Amen.

For further meditation read Song of Solomon 1:5.

Here now in our swiftly paced technological era, it seems to me that not only younger Black people, but we older ones as well, need urgently to show our living grandparents' generation that we do realize and respect and honor how much we have inherited and benefited because of the experience which they survived.

—Alex Haley

The black and white photos that capture highlights from the Civil Rights movement always remind me of my debt. Those photos immortalize the countless, and often nameless, persons who were brave enough to protest.

I remember the snapshot of protesters sitting patiently at segregated lunch counters while hecklers doused them with sugar and salt. Then there is the one of protesters splattered against brick buildings by the force of water cannons.

Today is a gift from them, and others brave like them. Somebody died that we might taste freedom. Somebody suffered that we could learn to read. Somebody welcomed tribulation that we could live like human beings.

We cannot afford to forget them or the God who empowered them. The temptation to forget looms large, the Scriptures tell us. Once our battles have seemingly been won and the foe is neutralized, we put God on the back burner.

Can you remember not to forget those God has used to bless you?

Dear God, help me treasure my foreparents and the bravery you instilled in them to make my today livable. Amen.

For further meditation read Deuteronomy 8:11-18.

Don't hate, it's too big a burden to bear.

—Martin Luther King, Sr.

Jesus commands us to love those who hate us. "Do good to those who hate you," he says. How is this possible? Hating those who despise us is like hitting those who strike us. Both are reflexes.

Daddy King preached love for decades. It is noble, and it is also common sense. Hate is heavy. Hating someone is like dragging around a cumbersome weight wherever we go. Hate is a hassle. It is awkward and bulky.

Jesus gives us the strength to love, but when we hate, we're out there by ourselves. He will have no part of that. Living in this world without hating is challenging but possible. We must allow God to rescue us from the temptation to retaliate.

Can you shun the heavy burden of hate and pick up love?

Dear God, I need your strength to help me love when I'd rather hate. Amen.

For further meditation read Luke 6:27-34.

I always wanted to be somebody. If I made it, it's half because I was game enough to take a lot of punishment along the way and half because there were a lot of people who cared enough for me.

—Althea Gibson

There is a flowering vine growing up the fence in my back-yard that I did not plant. The vine grows for two reasons. First, as a living thing, it has nature's drive to thrive. Second, the vine grows up the fence because it has something to lean on.

Like that plant, we also need a support system to help us grow upward. Yet possessing the people behind you is not enough. There must be an inner drive to achieve and accomplish as well. These two components often separate the half-steppers from the achievers. The Psalmist knew that his success was twofold, the gift of drive and of the people in his life. God gives us both components. The Psalmist once wrote, "If it had not been the Lord who was on our side . . .". Make use of both blessings and see how far you can go up.

Have you recognized the power of God at work in your success?

Dear God, you are the reason I succeed. Help me to see you more clearly in my life. Amen.

For further meditation read Psalm 124:1-8.

The ultimate measure of a man is not where he stands in moments of comfort and convenience, but where he stands at times of challenge and controversy.

—Martin Luther King, Jr.

As the popular saying goes, "When push comes to shove, you'll find out what you're made of." When we are at ease, everyone blends uniformly. Our encounters with the uncomfortable define us and show the world who we really are.

Though dreaded, the challenges of life test our mettle and clarify our values. Actually, they are good for us according to the Scriptures. "Suffering produces endurance, and endurance produces character, and character produces hope, and hope does not disappoint us."

Martin Luther King, Jr., went through this process most of his life. The world watched him take stands for or against one explosive topic after another. He must have known that hope was at the end of the trials and hope does not disappoint.

Are you in the midst of a defining moment?

Dear God, when I am tested, make me ready and unafraid. Amen.

For further meditation read Romans 5:3-5.

We must turn to each other and not on each other.

—Jesse L. Jackson

The teenage gang member interviewed on a television talk show spoke with little remorse. He said, "I shoot people because it's fun." I quickly condemned this youngster and mentally sentenced him to decades in reform school.

Rather than condemnation, that boy, like millions of other troubled youth, needs our concern. The best way out of the current youth crisis is to love them into correct living.

This young gang member was just one part of a huge and complicated problem that plagues our communities. Black-on-black crime, random violence, and drug abuse are other parts.

The problem is complex, but the answer is simple. Treat others the way you want to be treated. In times of distress we should be able to turn to each other for support, love, and understanding.

Can you be the listening post and concerned friend to a troubled person?

Dear God, when others around me experience difficulty, strengthen me to be there for them. Amen.

For further meditation read Proverbs 17:17.

The Reverend Jesse L. Jackson

To love is to make of one's heart a swinging door.

—Howard Thurman

This time my friend Kim had gone too far. She had abused our friendship and taken me for granted by losing the treasured doll I had loaned her. Although I was merely a child at the time, I devised a method of revenge.

I vowed to shut her and her carelessness out of my life by evicting my love for her from my heart. It seemed a plausible idea in my eight-year-old mind. With glee I placed an imaginary lock on my heart's door, an extra chain on the latch, and hung a "do not disturb sign" on the doorknob for the full effect. I meant business.

Later that same day, I shared with my mother my interior security measures. She patiently reminded me of a few things I'd done around the house that might have disappointed God. I panicked at the thought of God locking me out. There was excitement within me when I learned that we are forgiven time and time again. There are no locks on the heart of the Lord.

Can you keep your heart unlocked?

Dear God, locks have no place in the heart. Free me from the tendency to condemn. Amen.

For futher meditation read Matthew 18:21.

We ain't what we want to be; we ain't what we gonna be; but thank God, we ain't what we was.

—African American folk saying

We are like lumps of clay on the potter's wheel. God is the divine potter. God's hands are on us right now, molding and remolding who we are and who we should be.

While we are in the process of becoming God's finished product, let's celebrate what God has done thus far. Look back over your life. See the work of God. Think for a moment about the things you used to do. Reflect on those bad habits God enabled you to leave behind.

It's a blessing to be on the potter's wheel. It's good to have a God strong and patient enough to shape us and form us. God has smoothed out our defects and erased our flaws. God is just about to patch up our brokenness. We spend our entire lives on the potter's wheel. Our ancestors knew this and expressed the good news the best way they knew how.

Can you thank God for what God has done and for what God will do?

Dear God, keep your hands on me. Make me what you will. Amen.

For further meditation read Jeremiah 18:1-6.

Be not discouraged. There is a future for you. . . . The resistance encountered now predicates hope. . . . Only as we rise, do we encounter opposition.

—Frederick Douglass

These words exhorted our enslaved foreparents not to abandon their struggle for freedom. It seemed that the more they struggled, the more pain was inflicted upon them. In the face of certain pain, Douglass urged them to look toward the promised liberty.

They knew that God was their liberator and enabler. God was the one who made them brave in the face of danger and capable of dying for the cause they embraced. The slaves looked to God and saw their future.

Today we don't face slave masters and live on plantations as servants in fetters, but there are other situations equally as perilous. We need to look to God in order to see our tomorrow as well.

Those before us did not give up in the face of their trials. Let us not grow weary or lose heart. Our God is still in the blessing business.

Can you look beyond today's turmoil and see your future by keeping your eyes on God?

Dear God, my future is in your hands. Lead me to it with your power. Amen.

For further meditation read Galatians 6:9.

God does not bless us for nothing.

—Zan Holmes, Jr.

I wish I had a great singing voice. I often daydream about belting out songs with the vocal power of the unforgettable Mahalia Jackson. Sure, I have other gifts; but more than anything else, I wish I could sing.

Here I go, neglecting what I do have, as I yearn for what I lack. This attitude sounds a bit like the ungrateful servant Jesus spoke of in the parable of the talents, doesn't it? In the parable, the servant had been given a skill by God, but he wanted something else. Rather than using the skill he had, he complained about what he did not have. In the end, the complainer was punished by losing the one gift he did possess.

The talents and abilities we have were given to us because God ultimately knows what is best for us. God knows all about us. In fact, God knows us better than we know ourselves. Instead of complaining about what we lack, we should be glad for what we have and use it to the glory of God.

Can you trust God to bless you the way God wants to?

Dear God, thank you for what I have. Help me use it to your glory. Amen.

For further meditation read Matthew 25:14-30.

Lift every voice and sing
till earth and heaven ring,
ring with the harmonies of liberty;
let our rejoicing rise
high as the listening skies, . . .
Let us march on
till victory is won.

—James Weldon Johnson

Undeniably, music is in our bones. It is at the center of our being. Without a thought, fingers tap, feet pat, and maybe even bodies sway along with a syncopated tune. It's a natural reaction. We just can't help ourselves.

Our praise for God should also be a natural reaction. The remembrance of God in everything we say and do should flow from us automatically.

That's what the Psalmist meant, when he wrote: "Let everything that breathes praise the LORD!" We should let the praises to God flow, because we just can't help ourselves.

Can you praise God automatically throughout your day?

Dear God, let my praises to you flow like a never-ceasing stream. Amen.

For further meditation read Psalm 150:1-6.

James Weldon Johnson

There is no future for a people who deny their past.

—Adam Clayton Powell, Jr.

Kente cloth and African garb are currently the fashion rage. Many churches sponsor African attire Sundays, and the congregations as well as the pastors are decked out in the motherland's finest garb. In so doing we elevate our past, which makes the future all the more inviting. There is a divine connection between the past and the future. If we can tap into it, we can move ahead with power.

Our past is rich. In Africa we were architects and astronomers. In early America we were inventors and businesspersons. We inherit a legacy of overcoming and surviving. Our future is linked to those positive attributes. If we choose to deny them, there may be no future.

That's why the Psalmist spoke joyfully of what God had done—he knew that God would do it again and again. Our God does not go on vacation or take coffee breaks or noontime naps. "He will not let your foot be moved; he who keeps you will not slumber."

Can you celebrate the past as you walk toward the future?

Dear God, my past, present, and future are in your hands; keep on blessing me. Amen.

For further meditation read Psalm 121:1-8.

The fear that had shackled us all across the years left us suddenly when we were in that church together.

—Ralph David Abernathy

The church house has always been more than just four walls, a roof, and a floor. Church is our haven, our rock in the weary land, our place of refuge, and our shelter from the storm.

We've always been glad just to be there. That's why worship is usually punctuated with shouts of joy, laughter, and smiles. We know that for some of us, the journey that led to the church was a perilous one. For Abernathy and others who served with Dr. King, their very presence in the house of God was a blessing.

Once in God's house, our foreparents knew what to expect. Praises went up, and blessings came down. Burdens were lifted. Prayers were answered. Our challenge today is not to discount the power of God's holy ground. We can become so preoccupied with our superficial concerns that we miss the life-changing encounters with God in worship.

The spirit is willing; are you ready to truly worship when you visit God's house?

Dear God, free me from distractions so that I can meet you in worship. Amen.

For further meditation read Psalm 122:1.

I know one thing we did right
Was the day we started to fight.
Keep your eyes on the prize
Hold on . . .

—Civil Rights movement song

I can hear them singing this song as they marched for our freedom along some hot southern highway. They didn't know if snipers or cold lemonade would be waiting for them around the next bend, but they kept on marching anyway. They were undaunted by the dangers. They had set their minds on freedom, and no one was going to turn them around.

In our ever-changing world, a made-up mind is hard to find. Constant change is in. Steadfastness to purpose is out. Our fore-parents' ability to hold on still makes a difference in our lives today. We should thank God that they were strong in spirit and able to fight for the right.

The apostle Paul also had his mind made up. His eyes were on the prize too, and he refused to let it go until the goal was reached. Paul made Jesus his goal, and he vowed to press toward the goal no matter what it took.

Can you keep your eyes on the prize, which is Jesus?

Dear God, give me the steadfastness to march toward you and the goals that I have set.

For further meditation read Philippians 3:14.

We wanted something for ourselves and for our children, so we took a chance with our lives.

—Unita Blackwell

If you want to save your life, you've got to lose it, for Jesus' sake. That sounds scary, doesn't it? In reality, a life lost for the sake of Jesus means a life that is shared with other people. Such persons care more for others than for themselves.

Blackwell lost her life in a dream of a better day for African Americans. She found it as she worked toward that reality and helped others along the way. When you stop caring about yourself long enough to care about others, the spirit of the Lord abounds.

Jesus' words challenge us today to live selflessly in a me-oriented society. Also our challenge is to build up our community, preserving gains made thus far and laying foundations for the future God has for us.

Are you willing to lose so that you may gain?

Dear God, my humanness wants to hoard myself, my spirit wants to give.

For further meditation read Matthew 16:25.

I was conductor of the Underground Railroad for eight years, and I can say that I never ran my train off the track or lost a passenger.

—Harriet Tubman

It takes guts to be led. The life of an authentic follower is not easy. You must have complete trust in the leader. You must believe in the cause. You must follow instructions.

Tubman was a demanding leader. She never lost a passenger on her railroad because her passengers followed her lead in courage and in hope. Success on the Underground Railroad was due to their followership as well as her leadership.

The challenge we face today is truly following God. God will empower us if we can genuinely trust and obey. To trust God means we stop leaning on ourselves and lean on God. Trust in God means we realize that we are not God.

Are you brave enough to let the Lord truly lead you?

Dear God, give me the bravery to be led by you. Amen.

For further meditation read Proverbs 3:5.

Harriet Tubman

Don't pray when it rains if you don't pray when the sun shines.

—Leroy Satchel Paige

Would you call a friend only to complain? If you did, you wouldn't be much of a friend. Unfortunately, that's the way we treat God sometimes. God needs to hear from us at all times. We are expected to spend time with God throughout our day.

God is consistent. Our prayers should be also. The habit of praying only when we are in turmoil boxes God into one role in our lives. And God is much, much more. God is a mother, a father, a brother, and a sister. God is laughter in joy. God is tears in sadness.

Paige's words urge us to move into a constant communion with God. It is ongoing fellowship with the Lord that brings us steadiness and security of spirit.

Can you pray during the bad and the good times?

Dear God, I want to be able to pray to you always. Keep me mindful that you are ever listening. Amen.

For further meditation read 1 Thessalonians 5:17.

We know how bitter the cup is of which the slave hath to drink. Oh, how ought we to feel for those who yet remain in bondage!

—Richard Allen

Allen's plea for those brothers and sisters still trapped in slavery was heartrending. Life must have been bittersweet for the freed Blacks, because all were not free.

There is a similar dual life-style in our society today—those who recognize Jesus as the Savior, and those who know him not. If there were ever days in your life when you existed without the Lord, surely you know the "bitter cup" of life without the Savior. Life without Jesus is a bondage like no other.

Like Allen, we should be actively concerned about those bound by the ways of this world. We should not be comfortable with our lives until all are free in Jesus.

Have you experienced the liberating power of Jesus?

Dear God, many of those around me do not know your power. Use me to spread the truth to all. Amen.

For further meditation read John 8:32.

Invest in the human soul. Who knows, it might be a diamond in the rough.

—Mary McLeod Bethune

Jesus died on Calvary's cross because God believed we were worth the price. God was the world's best investor. God thought we might be diamonds in the rough, so God gave generously.

Bethune was also an investor. She took a trash dump, and with her concern she transformed it into Bethune-Cookman College. She invested in the future of young people because she believed they were worthy. She knew how to give of herself so that our people could excel.

Many others in this society are in dire need of someone to invest in them. They don't need vast amounts of capital to yield a return. Your genuine concern will do. Your personal involvement can turn little into much. Most of all, we need the love of God in our hearts if we are to invest in people. God's love makes us generous of spirit, of mind, and of possessions.

Can you give of yourself in the spirit of the Lord?

Dear God, allow your divine generosity to flow through me, that I might be a blessing to this world. Amen.

For further meditation read John 3:16.

MARY McLEOD BETHUNE

You may write me down in history
With your bitter, twisted lies,
You may trod me in the very dust
But still, like dust, I'll rise.

—Maya Angelou

The flexibility of the human spirit is phenomenal. You can twist it, stomp on it, cover it with dirt—but ultimately it will survive.

This reality explains our continued existence in America. We as a people possess an inner strength that makes us resilient and tough enough to survive ongoing adversities.

Truly it is something within us. According to the Bible, our power is "a treasure in an earthen vessel" from God. When cockiness takes hold of this gift, trouble sets in. When we start to give ourselves the glory—we forget that all our strength comes from the Lord. We must never forget God's goodness in our lives.

Can you remember the source of your strength?

Dear God, keep your powerful spirit in me that I may continue to rise, no matter what comes my way. Amen.

For further meditation read 2 Corinthians 4:7-10.

Look at me! Look at my arm! I have plowed and planted and gathered into barns, and no man could head me—and ain't I a woman? I could work as much and eat as much as a man (when I could get it) . . . and ain't I a woman? I have borne thirteen chillern and seen 'em mos' all sold off into slavery, and when I cried out with a mother's grief, none but Jesus heard—and ain't I a woman?

—Sojourner Truth

When the abused cower quietly in corners, injustice lives on. Bent heads, muffled voices, and terrified spirits invite wrongs to continue.

Though mistreated and devalued, Truth refused to keep quiet. Her reaction to wrong was to speak out. Her womanhood was slighted and her personhood was trampled, yet she traveled America to tell all who would listen about the evils of slavery.

Is it so wrong to want to be treated right? In our world today, sometimes we have to stand up and speak out. Silence is often compliance. We also should thank God for the gift of boldness of speech. It gives us the power to speak the truth even in the most oppressive situations.

Do you need God's boldness of speech today?

Dear God, open my mouth to address the wrongs of this world. Amen.

For further meditation read Acts 4:29.

I'll find a way or make one.

—Jackie Robinson

Consider the obstacles in your life as opportunities for miracles. First, obstacles are times to witness God's power at work. Second, obstacles are times to demonstrate your faith in God. If you can—God can.

As the first African American in major league baseball, Robinson was well acquainted with obstacles. He faced and conquered them at every turn. Had it not been for his overcoming attitude, the arena of athletics might not have been changed.

Jesus encourages us to think with such resolve. He said, "If you are able!—All things can be done for the one who believes." Everyone needs this relentless attitude for achievement.

Do you think you can?

Dear God, as I confront obstacles, remind me of your strength in order to bolster my faith. Amen.

For further meditation read Mark 9:23.

It must be borne in mind that the tragedy in life doesn't lie in not reaching your goal. The tragedy lies in having no goal to reach. It isn't a calamity to die with dreams unfulfilled, but it is certainly a calamity not to dream. It is not a disaster to be unable to capture your ideal, but it is a disaster to have no ideal to capture. Not failure, but low aim, is sin.

—Benjamin E. Mays

Lack of faith is the most destructive force on this earth. The tragedies in life of which Mays speaks occur because of a lack of faith in God and in the self. Without faith in anything, we are like ships tossed by the waves and the winds of the world. We wind up going nowhere fast.

Mays was a blessed man. Although he grew up dirt poor, he was rich because his parents loved him and nurtured him in Christian values. His faith in self and in God elevated him from sharecropper's son to president emeritus of Morehouse College.

Today we make the mistake of placing trust in material items, when the really valuable things are intangibles such as love, hope, trust, and faith. Our foreparents achieved greatly with less than we have today because they had more of what really counts. If we are to avoid tragedies such as the lack of achievement, we will seek to be more like them.

Can your faith in God be your motivation to succeed?

Dear God, I need you as my source of strength and power. Amen.

For further meditation read Matthew 21:22.

If you don't dream, you might as well be dead.

—George Foreman

Our dreams and hopes take us places we wouldn't ordinarily go. I'll bet it was in a dream that Rosa Parks first considered taking a seat in the white section of the public bus. A dream may have been the first time Douglas Wilder ever examined the idea of running for public office. Our dreams are open fields that know no boundaries.

Foreman, the boxer and the minister, knows all about the power that accompanies our dreams. His faith motivates him to achieve what might be perceived as impossible by others.

In our current society, it may seem foolish to dream. There are so many negative situations. Limitations are pronounced and boundaries are enforced. Yet, if we do not dare to dream we will become staid and stagnant. Our God works through our hopes and aspirations to move us ahead. We must fearlessly dream and hope in the name of the Lord.

Are you brave enough to dream?

Dear God, loosen the chains that keep me from seizing all that could be mine. Give me the courage to have faith that I can succeed. Amen.

For further meditation read Matthew 17:20.

No one rises to low expectations.

—Les Brown

Myra was a welfare mother who thought very little of herself. She and I were paired together for a mentoring program. Her task was to get off welfare and become self-sufficient. My task was to help her along the way.

When we first met, her low sense of self-esteem was obvious. Everything about her said, "I can't, I won't, I never will." I preached the importance of self-love to her until I was blue in my brown face. Nothing seemed to work. The lesson I learned was that Myra had to believe in herself. I could not do it for her. She needed to think about good things instead of concentrating on the bad. Once she began to free her mind from the negative, marvelous changes occurred in her life.

Paul also urges us to think on the good things. He knew that if we think on the positive, we will be inclined to act that way. As a people, many of us are paralyzed by negative events and occurrences. The way to free ourselves from the bad is to keep our minds on the good.

Are negative thoughts holding you prisoner?

Dear God, place my mind on what is good, what is positive, what is uplifting. Amen.

For further meditation read Philippians 4:8.

We wear the mask that grins and lies
It hides our cheeks and shades our eyes.

—Paul Laurence Dunbar

For centuries it was not safe for us to be our true selves. We kept our emotions in check. We played specific roles and hid behind masks. There was a danger in doing anything else but living behind the mask.

Grinning through our pain and lying about our true feelings were forced behaviors. We were locked into masks we did not want.

Poet Dunbar captured this sad reality in his poem to remind us of how it used to be. The Psalmist also wrote about a time of sadness. However, he included the good news with it: that a time of joy always accompanies the sad times. He wrote that "weeping may linger for the night, but joy comes with the morning."

Now we have the freedom to express ourselves. It is a joy to come from behind the masks and be the bright, expressive people that God has made us. We should celebrate that our society has changed for the better and that we serve a God who has ushered us into a new day.

Do you feel locked into a certain set of emotions?

Dear God, remove the fear I have to be the person that you have created. Amen.

For further meditation read Psalm 30:5.

My dad told me way back that you can't use race. For example, there's no difference between a white snake and a black snake. They'll both bite.

—Thurgood Marshall

Skin color has never been a reliable method of detecting whether a person is decent, upstanding, or moral. Being African American does not guarantee goodness. Neither does being white or any other color. Those who judge people by their color, like books by their covers, are in for trouble.

Like Marshall, I've discovered that our actions speak louder than our skin color ever could. Our actions reveal who we really are on the inside. They broadcast the genuine disposition of the heart.

Jesus knew this a long time ago, and he also urged people to look beyond the outer trappings. Jesus said, "You will know them by their fruits." A prejudiced person will bear the fruit of prejudice regardless of his or her color. A spiritual person will bear spiritual fruit. Let us look beyond the skin and to the actions in order to discern a person's intention.

What do your fruits say about you?

Dear God, help me live uprightly and produce godly acts. Amen.

For further meditation read Matthew 7:16-20.

Either we must attain freedom for the whole world or there will be no world left for any of us.

—Walter White

We need to look at the big picture, but selfishness gets in the way every time. White, a leader within the National Association for the Advancement of Colored People (NAACP), knew the destructiveness that selfishness was capable of. His words urge us to get ourselves out of the way and think about other people.

It is no small task to work for the freedom of the whole world. Small minds do slow down the process. The task is so large that it is bigger than all of our community-based organizations put together. However, the task is just the right size for God. The only way we can accomplish freedom for the world is by all laying our differences to the side and uniting in God.

Throughout the ages of time, when people have wanted to accomplish something of major importance, they turned to the Master, who empowered them to do great things. With God we can. Without God we can try and try and try, and fail.

Can you work toward something larger than yourself?

Dear God, make me aware of my responsibilities to care for others.

For further meditation read Philippians 2:3.

Let your motto be resistance, resistance, resistance! No oppressed people have ever secured their liberty without resistance.

—Henry Highland Garnet

If they had not resisted, where would we be today? Would iron fetters remain at our wrists and ankles? Would we still occupy slave quarters, and work from sunup to sundown in the cotton fields? Would we still bear the brunt of the master's whip?

Garnet's words urged our foreparents to hold fast to that which they believed and not to give up. Holding on to ideals and principles in times of distress is difficult at best. The stress and strain on them must have been overwhelming. Yet somehow they persevered.

Like them we also face the challenge of holding on to our ideals and principles. Our faith in God is challenged daily. We make decisions hourly based on our relationship with Christ. If we let go of that which we believe, what will be the fate of those who follow us?

Do you have the ability to actually live your faith?

Dear God, strengthen me as you did my ancestors, to fight the good fight and hold on to my beliefs.

For further meditation read 1 Timothy 6:11-12.

The problem of the twentieth century is the problem of the color line.

—William Edward Burghardt Du Bois

What should we do with the problems of our society? Racism, sexism, classism, ageism, and a host of other "isms" routinely confront us. Some people want to discuss and debate. Others respond with hate. Still more turn their disgust inward and are propelled by self-hate.

As a people, we have traditionally allowed society's problems with us to drive us out of our natural minds. If we plan to reach the future sane, the words from Paul may be the best advice.

Rather than react to what society does to us, with the power of God we can renew our minds and live lives that reflect the will of God. This means a calmness, an inner confidence, and joy in the face of adversity. There will be the ability to handle all that society taunts us with, not on their terms, but on God's terms.

Can you be renewed mentally and spiritually to meet the problems of our society?

Dear God, prepare me, your way, to deal with my world.

For further meditation read Romans 12:12.

Well, son, I'll tell you
Life for me ain't been no crystal stair.

—Langston Hughes

As the aroma of collard greens filled the air of my mother's kitchen, I tried desperately to escape to a room that offered fresh air to my lungs. No luck—the smell of the greens was everywhere, and there was no getting away from it.

I recall that event from childhood and see a connection between the love of an African American mother and the fragrance of those greens. Her love was strong and encompassing. When a black mother loves her child, there is no guessing about it. Her love sticks to her children everywhere they go. One can travel to the ends of the earth and feel that mother's love.

Hughes' poem depicts a conversation between a loving mother and her son. She lets him know that tough times are ahead of him. Also she tells him that she's already been through the difficult days, and if she can make it, so can he. Most of all, it is clear from their conversation that he is able to climb life's stairs because of her love for him. A mother's love is a gift from God.

Can the love of God within you empower others?

Dear God, thank you for making black mothers so strong and so loving.

For further meditation read 1 Corinthians 13.

It's a blessing to die for a cause, because you can so easily die for nothing.

—Andrew Young

When I read the newspaper headlines today, tears welled up in my eyes. Another young African American man was killed for his sneakers last night. As more and more lives are lost due to athletic shoes, gold chains, and leather jackets, we as a people must stop and take account of where we are headed. We are, in the words of Young, "easily dying for nothing."

His words hearken back to the way it used to be. Decades ago, young people put their lives on the line for the noble cause of racial equality. They fought racism, not one another. There was a unity and a sense of pride that kept our young folk looking ahead to a better day.

If anything, today's youth need a reason for living. Perhaps our youth care so little for life because there does not seem to be much to it. Jesus offers those who believe in him an "abundant life." Let us offer the life that comes from Jesus to this younger generation.

Are you a role model for the Christian life?

Dear God, our youth today are in need of a blessing. Give them purpose, hope, and your love.

For further meditation read John 10:10.

I try and tell them that the most wonderful thing in the world is to be who you are. That to be black is to shine and aim high.

—Leontyne Price

Don't give up on them. This young generation of ours is not hopeless. With their rap music, slang words, and creative hair cuts, we can love them still. In spite of their often offensive exteriors, they are wonderful and wondrous.

Let's realize it is hard to be young and African American today. The pitfalls they daily face are harrowing. Violence, drugs, and sex threaten to overtake the simple pleasures of just being a kid.

They need to hear a positive word from us today. Some encouragement, some praise, something to let them know you care, can make their self-esteem go sky high. When Jesus wanted to boost the self-esteem of others he told them how important they were to the world. Our youngsters are equally important; they are the "light of the world"; they should not be hidden.

Can you take the time to lift up a young person?

Dear God, help me to help a young person discover his or her worth in you.

For further meditation read Matthew 5:14.

You can make a lot of movies. You can win a lot of awards. But if you don't have God in your life, you don't have anything.

—Mr. T.

The media bombard us with larger-than-life images of athletes and actors in commercials. They fly through the air pushing high-priced shoes, or they drive expensive cars to portray the alleged good life. The message is clear: being rich is wonderful. However, is the message true? Millions of impressionable minds absorb what they see. They erroneously believe money and possessions are the keys to happiness.

Mr. T. offers a clear and concise message about the importance of material goods. The money, the fame, the possessions are ultimately meaningless. What really counts is a relationship with God.

Our challenge is to see beyond the media campaigns and realize that all that glitters is not gold. Also, we must understand that all that's popular is not of God. Our spiritual lives depend on our ability to see right from wrong.

Which is more important, the pursuit of material gain or the loss of your soul?

Dear God, help me make sense out of my world. Keep my values closely aligned with you.

For futher meditation read Matthew 16:26.

Subject Index

Quotation Index